TROPICAL RAIN FOREST
Habitats

By **Barbara Taylor**

GARETH**STEVENS**

GS

P U B L I S H I N G

A Member of the WRC Media Family of Companies

Please visit our web site at: www.garethstevens.com
For a free color catalog describing Gareth Stevens Publishing's
list of high-quality books and multimedia programs,
call 1-800-542-2595 or 1-800-387-3178 (Canada).
Gareth Stevens Publishing's fax: (414) 332-3567.

Library of Congress Cataloging-in-Publication Data

Taylor, Barbara, 1954-
  Tropical rain forest habitats / Barbara Taylor. – North American ed.
      p. cm. — (Exploring habitats)
  Includes bibliographical references and index.
  ISBN-10: 0-8368-7258-4 – ISBN-13: 978-0-8368-7258-3 (lib. bdg.)
  1. Rain forests—Juvenile literature. I. Title. II. Series.
QH86.T398   2007
578.734—dc22   2006044327

This North American edition first published in 2007 by
Gareth Stevens Publishing
A Member of the WRC Media Family of Companies
330 West Olive Street, Suite 100
Milwaukee, WI 53212 USA

This U.S. edition copyright © 2007 by Gareth Stevens, Inc. Original
edition copyright © 2002 by ticktock Entertainment Ltd. First published
in Great Britain in 1999 by ticktock Publishing Ltd., Unit 2, Orchard
Business Centre, North Farm Road, Tunbridge Wells, Kent, TN2 3XF.

Gareth Stevens editor: Richard Hantula
Gareth Stevens designer: Charlie Dahl
Gareth Stevens managing editor: Mark J. Sachner
Gareth Stevens art direction: Tammy West
Gareth Stevens production: Jessica Morris

Picture Credits: t=top, b=bottom, c=centre, l=left, r=right, OFC=outside
front cover, OBC=outside back cover, IFC=inside front cover

B&C Alexander; 28/29c, 29cr. Bruce Coleman Limited; 12/13b, 14tr, 20tl.
Colorific; 3c. Jacana; 2tl, 6bl, 7tr, 7br, 8cr, 10/11t, 11tr, 12tl, 13r, 14bl, 17tr,
18c, 18/19c, 19b, 21br, 26/27c, 27b, 31br & OFC. Oxford Scientific Films;
IFC, 12br, 19tc, 22tl, 24br, 26tl. Planet Earth Pictures; OFC (main pic), 2l &
2bl, 3/4b, 3tr, 3/4t, 4/5t, 4/5c, 4/5b, 5br, 6br, 6c, 6tr, 7bl, 8tl, 8tr, 8c, 8br, 9t,
9c, 9cr, 10l, 10tl, 11c, 11b, 14/15b, 15br & OBC, 16tl, 16bl, 17c & 32, 17b,
18tl, 18bl, 19tr, 20bl, 20cr, 21tl, 21c, 21tr, 22c, 22cl, 22/23ct, 23tr, 23cl, 23br,
24/25c, 24bl, 25tr, 25br, 26l & 26bl, 26/27t, 27t, 28tl, 28bl, 29br & OBC,
30tl, 30bl, 30/31c, 31tr. P.I.X; 15t. Tony Stone; 29cl.

Printed in the United States of America

1 2 3 4 5 6 7 8 9 10 09 08 07 06

CONTENTS

SNAKES OF
THE FOREST

Eyelash pit vipers come in all
sorts of colors, from yellow and
orange to green and purple. They
are named after the hornlike
scales over their eyes.

THE LIVING FOREST

Imagine walking through a warm, damp, dark forest where huge trees form a green roof that shuts out the sky. The buzzing of insects fills the air, and occasionally you glimpse a bird or a monkey high in the treetops. This is what a tropical rain forest is like. At least half of all the animal and plant species in the world live in tropical rain forests, including, by some estimates, at least 30 million different insects. The main reasons for this incredible richness are a warm, wet climate year-round and constant competition to find living space and avoid predators. People often call tropical rain forests jungles, from the Hindi *jangal*, meaning the thick forest that grows after the original forest is cleared.

CANOPY CREATURES

In the busy, bustling world of the canopy, the tree branches form a convenient high-level walkway used by many animals, such as the howler monkey (*above*). Fruit bats and birds fly through the leaves and branches.

LAYERS OF LIFE

A tropical rain forest has four main layers.

THE EMERGENT LAYER
Some giant trees, called emergents, grow beyond the top floor of the forest.

THE CANOPY
Most rain forest life is found in the canopy, some 130 feet (40 meters) above the ground. This layer receives the most rain and sunshine, and so contains the most food, such as leaves, flowers, and fruits.

THE UNDERSTORY
Between the canopy and the forest floor is an understory of smaller trees, climbing plants, and large-leaved shrubs that can tolerate the shade.

THE FOREST FLOOR
Only 1 or 2 percent of the sunlight that hits the canopy filters through to the forest floor. The ground is almost bare except for a thin carpet of leaves.

FOREST GIANTS

The year-round warmth of the tropical rain forest has allowed some animals to grow into giants, such as the giant millipedes (*left*). These look rather alarming but actually feed on dead plant material. Other rain forest giants include the largest frog in the world, the goliath frog, and the largest butterfly, the Queen Alexandra's birdwing butterfly.

FOREST PEOPLES

The Kalapalo Indians (*right*) are among the peoples living in the Brazilian rain forest. Humans have inhabited tropical rain forests for thousands of years, but little is known of their origins, their relationship to one another, or how they colonized the forest. Warmth and moisture break down organic materials, such as wood, very quickly, so ancient remains are rare.

LIFE IN THE UNDERSTORY

Among the tangle of leaves and branches in the understory live climbing and grasping animals. Many are small and light, such as tree frogs, lemurs, coatis, and tree snakes like the emerald tree boa (*above*). Others are much heavier and have to keep to the larger branches.

THE FOREST FLOOR

Large hunters such as jaguars and tigers prowl along the forest floor. Hogs, peccaries, and tapirs can root out bulbs and shoots from the soil, and there are plenty of insects for hungry giant anteaters and tenrecs.

TROPICAL RAIN FORESTS OF THE WORLD

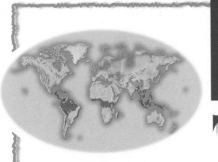

WHERE IN THE WORLD?

Today, four main areas of the world contain tropical rain forest (shaded dark green *above*): Central and South America, Africa, Southeast Asia, and Australasia (Australia and nearby islands). Every tropical rain forest is different, with many species of plants and animals living only in one area. This is because the continents drifted apart over millions of years, separating the various areas of rain forest so that the plants and animals developed separately into different forms.

The term rain forest was first used in 1898 to describe forests that grow in wet conditions. A few rain forests exist in regions with a temperate climate, but most are tropical rain forests, located in tropical parts of the world. These forests tend to have an annual rainfall of at least 100 inches (250 centimeters), spread throughout the year. Thunderstorms are common in the afternoons. Water given off by the trees adds to the moisture in the air, so the air feels sticky, or humid, and clouds and mist hang over the forest like smoke. This cloud blanket protects the forest from daytime heat and nighttime chill, keeping temperatures between 73° Fahrenheit (23° Celsius) and 88°F (31°C) throughout the year. The hottest, wettest rainforests occur in a belt along the Equator. These are sometimes called lowland rain forests, and they are the most extensive. Rain forests further away from the Equator are just as warm as lowland rain forests but have a short dry season. Another type of rain forest, called cloud forest, grows on tropical mountains, while mangrove rain forests grow on some tropical coasts.

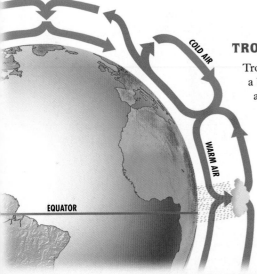

COLD AIR

WARM AIR

EQUATOR

TROPICAL RAIN FOREST CLIMATE

Tropical rain forests are hot because they grow in a band along the Equator where the Sun's rays are at their hottest and strongest. The Sun's heat warms the ground, which then warms the air above it. The warm air rises up. As it rises, it cools down, and moisture in the air condenses into water droplets, which collect together to make clouds and rain (*left*).

MONSOON OR SEASONAL FORESTS

Tropical rain forests with three or more dry months each year are called monsoon forests or seasonal forests (*left*). In these the trees drop their leaves in the dry season and grow new leaves at the start of the wet monsoon season. These forests have fewer climbing plants than lowland tropical rain forests because the air is drier. There are also more plants growing on the forest floor because a lot of light reaches the ground in the dry season.

CLOUD FORESTS

High up on tropical mountains – above 3,000 feet (900 m) – grow misty forests of gnarled, twisted, stunted trees covered in bright green mosses and dripping with water. Lichens hang down like beards from the tree branches, and ferns, orchids, and other plants perch along the boughs. These cloud (or montane) rain forests (*left*) have fewer plant species than lowland forests, as relatively low temperatures and strong winds restrict plant growth.

THE WATER CYCLE

As rain drips down through the rain forest, the trees and plants take in moisture through their leaves and roots. Unused water evaporates, or disappears, into the air through tiny holes in their leaves. Water also evaporates from the ground. All the warm, wet air rises up into the sky, where it cools down to make rain clouds. Rain falls down from the clouds into the forest to start the rainfall cycle (*above*) all over again.

MANGROVE FORESTS

Tropical shorelines are often clothed in a special type of rain forest, called a mangrove forest (*left*), which does not have a great variety of species. These forests grow on the coasts of the Indian Ocean, the western Pacific Ocean, and also on the shores of the Americas, the Caribbean, and West Africa.

WHAT'S THE WEATHER?

Inside a tropical rain forest, the local climate, or microclimate, varies at different levels, so animals (*right*) on the forest floor experience different conditions from those in the canopy. When it rains, the water drips down through the leaves, sometimes taking ten minutes to reach the ground. When the Sun shines, the air at the top of the canopy is hot and dry, but on the ground it is always warm and damp. A strong wind may be blowing up in the canopy, but at ground level there isn't even a breeze.

ASIAN RAIN FORESTS

Almost 40 percent of all the tropical rain forest in Asia (*above*) is to be found in the Indonesian archipelago, including Borneo, and most of the richest mangrove forests occur along Southeast Asian coasts.

ASIA

The main area of tropical rain forest in Southeast Asia spreads down the mainland of Malaysia to Indonesia. Widespread human disturbance of the forests of mainland Southeast Asia has left little of the rain forest in its natural state. Some islands, such as the Philippines, have hardly any rain forest left. Because of this, many Asian rain forest species are in danger of extinction, such as the Sumatran rhinoceros and the Vietnamese pheasant. Other areas, such as Borneo, still have much of their original forest cover.

ATLAS MOTH

The Atlas moth (*left*) is one of the largest moths in the world. It has a wingspan of up to 12 inches (30 cm) and is often mistaken for a bird as it flutters around the tropical rain forests of Southeast Asia. Males have huge feathery antennae – the largest of any butterfly or moth – to help them pick up the scent of females among the trees.

MANGROVE TREES

Mangrove trees (*left*) grow in salty, silty mud and have a tangle of branching roots to support them in the waterlogged ground. Special breathing roots stick up through the mud into the air to help the roots get enough oxygen. The roots also trap the mud and help stabilize the coastline and build up new strips of land.

KING COBRA

The largest of all venomous, or poisonous, snakes are king cobras (*right*), which can grow as long as 18 feet (5.5 m). They are actually shy snakes and prefer to keep well away from people. Female king cobras are the only snakes known to build a nest for their eggs.

MALAYAN TAPIR

The black and white colors of the Malayan tapir (*left*) help break up its outline so predators cannot see it in the dark. Tapirs are shy, timid, solitary animals and come out mainly at night. They use their long trunklike nose to pull tender shoots, buds, and fruits from rain forest plants.

AUSTRALASIA

AUSTRALASIAN RAIN FORESTS

Australasian tropical rain forests (*above*) spread up from the northeastern coast of Queensland in Australia to the island of New Guinea.

The largest expanse of tropical rain forest in Australasia (the region encompassing Australia and nearby islands) grows on the island of New Guinea. Most of it is still undisturbed and contains a mixture of Asian and Australasian plants and animals. Small areas in northern Australia are all that remain of a vast tropical rain forest that once covered parts of this continent and Antarctica during much warmer climates millions of years ago. Although not as rich in species as other rain forests, they contain many unique forms of life.

SPOTTED CUSCUS

Several species of cuscus, including the spotted cuscus (*left*), live in the rain forests of New Guinea. Cuscuses have a partly bald prehensile, or gripping, tail for grasping branches. At night they feed on leaves, flowers, and insects; some species feed in the rain forest canopy, others in the understory or on the ground.

TREE KANGAROOS

Australasian rain forests do not have monkeys and apes climbing and swinging through the trees. Instead, they have tree kangaroos (*left*) and a variety of other marsupials, such as possums and gliders. Tree kangaroos live mainly on New Guinea, but two species live in Queensland rain forests. Tree kangaroos are different from ground-dwelling kangaroos because they have powerful front legs, relatively short, broad back feet, sharp claws for gripping branches, and a long, cylindrical tail. The long tail helps a tree kangaroo keep its balance on tree branches, and also acts as a rudder when it leaps from branch to branch.

RAINBOW LORIKEET

Screeching flocks of rainbow lorikeets (*above*) feed in the upper canopy of the forest, lapping up nectar and pollen from flowers with their brush-tipped tongues. They may have to fly long distances in search of flowering trees.

AFRICA

African tropical rain forests contain fewer species than those of the Americas or Asia. This is because many plants and animals died out when the climate of Africa became much drier during the last Ice Age, which ended about 10,000 years ago. Most of the wildlife in Madagascar's rain forests is unique to the island because it has evolved in isolation from Africa for tens of millions of years.

AFRICAN RAIN FORESTS

A belt of tropical rain forest grows across the center of Africa (*above*), from Cameroon and Gabon on the West African coast, to Kenya and Tanzania in East Africa. More than 80 percent of Africa's rain forest is in central Africa. These forests spread out from small patches of forest that survived the dry African climate during the last Ice Age. In East Africa, rain forest grows mainly in mountain regions.

GOLIATH BEETLE

The heaviest of all insects, male goliath beetles (*left*) weigh 2.5 to 3.5 ounces (70 to 100 grams), which is roughly three times as much as a house mouse. From the tip of the small horns to the end of the abdomen, they are up to 4 inches (11 cm) long. Females are smaller than males.

THE SAME BUT DIFFERENT

Animals living in rain forests in different parts of the world sometimes look the same because they have adapted to a similar lifestyle. They are different species, but because they live, feed, and survive in a similar way, their bodies look similar. This idea is called convergent evolution, and one example is the hornbills of Africa (*above*) and the toucans of South America (*below*).

COLOBUS MONKEY

Living in troops that may number more than 50 animals and are made up of small family groups, black-and-white colobus monkeys (*right*) are active during the daytime. They feed on bark, insects, fruit, and leaves, leaping acrobatically from tree to tree. Unlike South American monkeys, African monkeys do not have prehensile tails.

AFRICAN GRAY PARROT

Noisy African gray parrots (*left*) whistle and shriek to each other before settling down to roost for the night in groups of 100 or more. They have remarkable powers of mimicry, and captive birds can be trained to use human language as a means of communicating intelligently with people.

THE AMERICAS

By far the biggest area of tropical rain forest is in the Amazon basin in South America. It is twice the size of India and ten times the size of France. By some estimates about one-fifth of all the world's bird and flowering plant species and one-tenth of all its mammal species live in the Amazon rain forest. Each type of tree may support, on average, more than 400 insect species.

WESTERN HEMISPHERE RAIN FORESTS

The tropical rain forests of the Americas range from the vast forests of the Amazon up through Central America and on to some of the islands in the Caribbean. These islands have many unusual species – some found on only one island. Hurricanes, however, often cause damage to the Caribbean rain forests. The relatively tiny rain forests of Central America are rich in species because they grow on a land bridge between two very different continents.

YELLOW ANACONDA

The yellow anaconda (*left*) is one of the heaviest snakes. It is highly aquatic, hunting fish and caimans in streams and rivers. Anacondas are a type of boa and constrict their prey, squeezing it to death in their strong coils.

BALD UAKARI

With its rather bare face, long shaggy fur, and a beard, the bald uakari (*right*) is a strange-looking monkey indeed. It and other species of uakari are the only New World monkeys to have short tails. Uakaris rarely leap, because they do not have long tails to help them keep their balance.

MORPHO BUTTERFLY

The shimmery blue colors on the wings of a male morpho butterfly (*right*) help attract females and may also serve to dazzle predators when the butterfly needs to escape. The colors are caused by the way the tiny scales on the wings reflect light.

TROPICAL RAIN FOREST PLANTS

Trees form the superstructure of a tropical rain forest. Their crowns make roof gardens for perching plants; their mighty trunks support the weight of the canopy and provide climbing frames for ropelike creepers; and their roots help hold the soil together. Rain forest trees are usually 100-160 feet (30-50 m) tall and have slender, unbranched trunks, smooth bark, and hard wood. Their life span can be from 150 years to 1,400 years. The leaves of rain forest trees and other rain forest plants are often thick and leathery. Many have pointed tips called drip tips. The rain runs quickly off these leaves, thereby keeping moss from growing and blocking out the light. A rain forest has a huge variety of trees – an area of about 2.5 acres (1 hectare) may hold as many as 200 species.

A SAFE HAVEN

To get nearer the Sun's light, plants known as epiphytes perch high on the branches of tall trees. Some of these plants, called bromeliads, make a cup-shaped container with their waxy leaves, which can hold many gallons of water. Animals such as frogs (*above*) may use these treetop ponds as safe places for their young.

GROWING SPACE

One of the main problems for rain forest trees is finding space in which to grow. Strangler figs (*left, right*) solve this problem by taking the place of a tree that is already standing.

A bird drops a strangler fig seed on a tree branch, and the seed sprouts roots and branches.

The strangler's roots reach the ground, and it starts to smother the host tree.

The host tree dies away, leaving the fig standing in its place.

STINKBIRDS

The hoatzin (*left*) of South America smells rather like cow manure because its stomach is full of fermenting leaves. It is one of the few rain forest birds to feed on leaves, which stay in the hoatzin's stomach for almost two days, making it too heavy to be a good flier.

CARNIVOROUS PLANTS

Pitcher plants (*left*) get extra nutrients by catching and digesting insects and other small animals. Some pitchers rest on the ground, while others hang like lanterns along the branches of supporting trees. Some even have lids to keep out the rain. Creatures are attracted by the glistening colors and sweet nectar produced around the rim of the pitcher, but they fall down the slippery walls into a pool of liquid. The liquid digests the animals' bodies, and the plant absorbs the nutrients they contain.

BUTTRESS ROOTS

The roots of some trees spread out above the ground to form wide, flat wings called buttresses (*right*). These buttress roots may extend as high as 16 feet (5 m) up the trunk. They probably help support tall trees, but may also help the trees to feed. They spread widely and send down fine feeding roots into the soil.

PARASITIC PLANTS

Plants need light to make food, but there is not much light on the dark forest floor. Some plants survive there by stealing food from other plants. The biggest flower in the world, rafflesia (*left*), is such a parasitic plant. The body of the plant is a network of threads living inside the woody stem of a vine that hangs down from the trees and trails along the ground. The flower bud pushes its way out through the vine's bark and then expands to form a flower up to 3 feet (1 m) across.

AVOCADO BIRD

The resplendent quetzal (*above*) feeds on several different species of avocado, and the trees and the birds need each other to survive. The quetzals swallow the avocado fruit whole but the hard seed passes through the bird's gut unharmed or is regurgitated later. A new tree can grow from the seed, so the quetzal spreads avocado trees through the forest. If the avocado trees are cut down or stop fruiting, quetzals usually disappear from the area.

PLANT PARTNERS

Most flowering plants in a tropical rain forest need pollen from another plant of the same kind in order to produce seeds. There is very little wind, so they rely on animals to transport the pollen. Highly mobile animals such as birds, bats, and monkeys are useful for spreading seeds, since they move over large areas of the forest. Flowers and seeds may sprout directly from trunks or branches to make contact more easily with bats and other large animals, without all the leaves getting in the way. Bat flowers tend to be large, pale, and smelly so bats can find them in the dark, while bird flowers show brilliant colors because birds have good color vision. Some insects, especially ants, have more complex relationships with rain forest plants – they live right inside the plants and help them survive.

PERFUME FOR POLLEN

The bucket orchid of Central America goes to extraordinary lengths to make sure iridescent male bees carry its pollen from flower to flower. To lure bees into its watery trap, the bucket orchid produces a perfume that the male bees use to attract females during courtship. While scraping perfume off the orchid's petals, the bees sometimes slip and fall down into the bucket (*above*). As they escape, they either pick up a new load of pollen or deposit pollen they are already carrying. The two lumps stuck to the bee's back like a yellow knapsack (*right*) are pollen.

SPREADING SEEDS

Living inside the stems, branches, and even leaves of several rain forest plants are colonies of ants. In exchange for their protected nesting place, the ants provide the plants with much-needed nutrients in their droppings and the remains of their insect meals. Ant plants are often epiphytes, perched high on tree branches, so they cannot get nutrients from the soil to help them grow. The ants may also defend the plants by biting and stinging animals that try to eat them. This ant plant (*left*) has holes in the surface of its swollen, prickly stem, through which its ant lodgers scurry in and out of their living home. As the ants move about the forest, they help spread the seeds of the ant plant.

GREEN FUR

The greenish tinge of the sloth's fur (*right*) is provided by tiny photosynthetic organisms called cyanobacteria that live in grooves in the damp hair. Since sloths never clean their fur, the bacteria do not get washed off, and they benefit by living high in the trees, near the light. With green fur, sloths blend into the leafy green background of the forest – the bacterial hitchhikers camouflage them from predators. Another creature takes advantage of the sloth-cyanobacteria relationship – a tiny moth lays its eggs in the sloth's green fur, and its caterpillars seem to feed on the cyanobacteria.

BEETLE MESSENGERS

To attract beetles for pollination, the philodendron (*left*) produces a powerful scent that travels great distances. The flowering spike even heats up to help the scent evaporate and disperse into the air. The beetles feed and mate inside the flower, then fly away covered with pollen, to another philodendron flower.

MOVING THROUGH THE TREES

FLYING LIZARD

In the Southeast Asian tropical rain forests, lizards are some of the most common gliders (*above*). Their stiff gliding flaps are made of thin membranes of skin joined to their ribs. These lizards can glide for up to 50 feet (15 m) between trees, and can even change position and roll over while in the air. Since gliders make easy targets for hungry birds, many are camouflaged or come out at night when it is harder for predators to see them on the move.

Even with special climbing equipment, people find it difficult and dangerous to reach the tops of tropical rain forest trees. Yet rain forest animals spend their lives swinging, climbing, and gliding through the trees. Useful adaptations developed in these forest acrobats include long arms for swinging, tails for gripping, hanging, and balancing, and sticky toes, rough soles, or long claws for a better grip. Short, rounded wings help predatory birds twist and turn through branches, while hummingbirds and moths hover in front of flowers on their small, pointed wings like jet aircraft. Some animals glide from tree to tree instead of leaping and travel long distances with very little effort. Webs or flaps of skin increase the body's surface area and slow down the glider's fall, like a living parachute. There is even a flying snake that can glide up to 165 feet (50 m).

CLINGING CLAWS

The long, strong claws of a sloth (*left*) work like hooks to allow the animal to spend much of its time hanging upside down from the branches of trees – even when it is asleep or dead. The claws make a rigid, fixed hook over the tree branches. The sloth's sluggish lifestyle requires very little effort and contrasts strongly with the speedy swinging of monkeys and apes.

GRIPPING TAILS

A variety of rain forest animals, from tree porcupines and tree anteaters to kinkajous and woolly monkeys, have a prehensile tail that can curl around branches like a hook. Such a tail is most highly developed in South American monkeys (*right*). For some unknown reason, the monkeys of Africa and Southeast Asia evolved without this useful adaptation. Most monkeys with prehensile tails use them as a fifth limb, for holding and gathering their food, as well as for moving.

HAIRY SWINGER

With their long arms and strong fingers and toes, orangutans *(above)* move easily through the trees, using their feet as well as their hands for climbing. To travel fast, they swing hand over hand, a technique called "brachiating." Older male orangs are too heavy to do this, but females and young are adept at treetop travel, sometimes walking along branches as well as brachiating. A female orangutan may have an arm span as great as 8 feet (2.4 m) and can cover large distances quickly.

GLUED TO THE SPOT

Tree frogs, such as the red-eyed tree frog *(right)*, have special pads under the toes that produce a sticky substance called mucus. Their sticky toes help them grip wet leaves and other slippery and slimy surfaces as they climb through the trees.

JAGUAR

COLLARED PECCARY

GRASS, ROOTS, BULBS, AND WORMS

One of the many links between rain forest plants and animals is through their feeding habits. Food chains generally start with plants because they make their own food, and then the plant eaters (herbivores) in turn are eaten by meat eaters (carnivores).

HIDDEN KILLER

Curled up among the leaves of the forest floor, the gaboon viper is well camouflaged as it waits for a tasty small animal to wander past. Then it leaps out and grabs hold of its prey in a surprise attack (*above*). Gaboon vipers kill their prey by biting it with their poisonous fangs. They have the longest fangs of any snake – each one is up to 2 inches (5 cm) long. A snake's teeth are good for holding prey, but not for chopping or chewing, so snakes swallow their prey whole.

PREDATORS AND PREY

R ain forest predators are mostly small animals because there are not enough large plant eaters in the forest to sustain large meat eaters. The exceptions to this are the large cats, such as the jaguar and the tiger, which hunt pigs, antelope, and deer on the forest floor. Ground-dwelling snakes also lie in wait for their prey on the forest floor, while their tree-dwelling relatives lurk among the branches. Other ground predators include troops of bush dogs in South America and sloth bears in southern India and Sri Lanka. High-level hunters include the fierce hawks and eagles that swoop down into the canopy to sieze monkeys and sloths with their strong talons.

TERRIBLE TEETH

Some piranha fish, such as red-bellied piranhas, are lethal killers, carving slices of flesh from their victims with razor-sharp teeth (*left*). They have powerful jaws that snap together in a strong bite. Meat-eating piranhas have been known to attack animals as large as goats that have fallen into the water. But all piranhas can eat fruit and nuts, and some are completely vegetarian.

SNAPPING JAWS

The caimans (*right*) of Central and South America have sharper, longer teeth than their relatives, the alligators. They lurk in the water, waiting to snap up fish, frogs, or thirsty animals that come down to the rain forest rivers for a drink. Caimans have strong, bony plates in their back and belly scales for protection against their own predators.

TONGUE ZAPPER

Insects are a major source of food for many tropical rain forest predators, from birds and bats to tarantulas and chameleons. Chameleons flick out their incredibly long tongue at lightning speed to trap insects, spiders, scorpions, and other prey with its sticky tip (*above*). To search for food, a chameleon can swivel its eyes in all directions. Its movements can be so slow that they are hardly noticeable, especially since the chameleon can change color to blend with its surroundings.

FELINE HUNTER

Small, agile forest cats, such as the South American margay (*right*), are skilled climbers that prey on small rodents, birds, and lizards in the trees. Most of them are nocturnal hunters, and their yellow or brownish fur with spotted or striped markings gives them good camouflage. Keen sight, hearing, and smell enable them to track down their victims, which they kill with a bite to the neck with their sharp, pointed teeth.

FOOD CHAIN

BENTWING BAT

⬇

INSECTS

⬇

FLOWERS

This food chain from an Australian rain forest has three links. Should any link be destroyed, it will affect the rest of the chain, and all the other food chains in the large and complex food web.

DEFENSE

From armor and camouflage to weapons and poisons, rain forest animals use all kinds of defensive tactics to avoid being eaten. Sometimes it is possible to run, leap, fly, or glide away from a predator, but hiding or blending in with the background is often more successful. Many rain forest insects look just like leaves, twigs, or bark, and as long as they keep still, they are hard to detect. Certain spiders even disguise themselves as bird droppings. Poisonous animals tend to have bright warning colors to tell predators to keep away. Some nonpoisonous butterflies copy the colors of poisonous species to trick predators. Another way animals may defend themselves is by putting up a fight.

ANGRY PIGS

The giant forest hog (*above*) is the largest wild pig and is feared by forest peoples for its unpredictable temper. It has well developed lower canine teeth that stick out of the sides of the mouth to form tusks. Males have larger tusks than females.

SPIDER SURVIVAL

This tarantula (*right*) is trying to make itself look as frightening as possible to scare predators away. Spiders use their poisonous fangs for defense, and tarantulas also flick irritating hairs at attackers. A few spiders look just like stinging insects such as wasps or ants, so predators are tricked into leaving them alone. Spiders will even pretend to be dead, since predators prefer to eat living prey.

HIDE AND SEEK

Insects are a major source of food in the rain forest, so they have developed a huge variety of unusual colors, patterns, and shapes to pretend they are not nice, tasty snacks. Dead leaves are a good disguise to adopt, and leaf insects often have veins and tattered edges just like the real thing (*left*).

FALSE EYES

Some camouflaged butterflies and moths have a second line of defense if they are disturbed by a predator. They suddenly open their front wings to reveal bright colors (called flash colors) and markings on their back wings (*right*). The markings may look like the eyes of a rain forest cat or snake. This sudden display startles the predator, making it hesitate long enough for the butterfly or moth to escape.

TREE DEFENSE

To deter leaf-eating insects, the rubber tree produces a milky latex that hardens into a sticky gum. This sticks the insects' mouthparts together and prevents them from eating the tree. The latex is the raw material for making rubber. It is collected by making slanting cuts in the bark. The latex oozes slowly from the cuts and is collected in a cup fixed to the tree trunk (*above*). The bark gradually heals, and the trees can be tapped again and again over a number of years.

BODY ARMOR

Pangolins, or scaly anteaters, are protected by a covering of horny skin scales that overlap like the tiles on a roof (*left*). When the pangolin curls tightly into a ball, the scales form a tough shield which only the larger cats can bite through. Pangolins eat ants and termites and their body armor helps protect them from insect bites and stings as well as from predators.

FROG POISONS

Poison dart frogs (*below*) secrete deadly poisons in their skin and are brightly colored to warn potential predators to keep away. They make some of these poisons themselves but also obtain some from their food, such as toxic insects. The frogs' poisons are so powerful that a tiny smear is enough to kill a horse. A few Amazonian tribes use this poison on the tips of their blowpipe darts for hunting.

NIGHTTIME ANIMALS

As darkness falls swiftly over a tropical rain forest, squeaks, scratchings, and rustlings fill the night air. The forest becomes dimly lit by moonlight, flashing fireflies, or glowing fungi. As much as 80 percent of all animal activity in a rain forest takes place at night. The darkness hides animals from their enemies, while the cool, moist night air suits insects and amphibians. Nighttime, or nocturnal, animals live in all parts of the rain forest. Deer, okapis, and armadillos roam the forest floor while tarsiers, bush babies, bats, moths, and small jungle cats move through the trees. Some flowers open up specially at night so they can be pollinated by nocturnal animals. To find their way in the dark, nocturnal animals have special senses, such as huge eyes or very sensitive ears and noses. Some snakes, called pit vipers, can pick up the heat given off by birds and mammals and use this to track their prey in the dark.

BAT CONVEYANCE

Rain forest bats, such as the long-tongued bat (*above*), fly through the forest at night searching for nectar, fruit, and insects. As they visit forest flowers, bats help spread the flowers' pollen and their seeds, so bats and the plants help each other survive.

SLOW MOVERS

Pottos (*right*) move very slowly and deliberately through a tree so their movements go undetected. If a potto hears the slightest sound or unexpected movement, it will suddenly freeze until it feels the danger has passed. It can stay "frozen" like this for hours if necessary, but the technique works well in very thick, leafy vegetation.

NIGHT CAMOUFLAGE

The spotted markings of the clouded leopard (*left*) help it hide when it is hunting at night because they break up the outline of its body among the leaves and branches of the forest trees. Clouded leopards hunt by pouncing from tree branches as well as by stalking prey on the ground.

TOAD INVASION

The cane toad of South America has been introduced into the rain forests of northeastern Australia. The spotted-tailed quoll (*left*) hunts and kills the toad but, unfortunately, is killed by the poison in the toad's skin and so the quolls' numbers have fallen drastically. The toad has no natural predators in Australia because it comes from a different region of the world, so its numbers are increasing.

NIGHT MONSTER

The rare aye-aye of Madagascar (*above*) has huge ears like a bat, big eyes like an owl, and a bushy tail like a squirrel. But its scariest feature is its long, spindly middle finger. The animal listens for the sound of insect larvae moving inside branches and tree trunks and digs them out with its creepy finger (*below*). Unlike other primates (monkeys, apes, lemurs, bush babies, and humans), the aye-aye has claws instead of nails on its fingers and toes.

EYES AND EARS

The huge, batlike ears of the lesser bush baby (*right*) help it track the movements of its insect prey in the darkness. Insects may even be snatched out of the air as they fly past. The large eyes let in as much light as possible, and there is a special layer called a "tapetum" at the back of the eye to reflect light back into the eye. This is what makes the bush babies' eyes shine in the dark.

PHEASANT FEATHERS

To impress a female, the male argus pheasant spreads out his stunning wing feathers, making an enormous fan (*above*). He clears a space on the forest floor and struts up and down, calling loudly to attract a female. Argus pheasants live in the tropical rain forests of Southeast Asia.

COURTSHIP

In most tropical rain forests, the weather stays the same all the time, and so there are no definite breeding seasons. The timing of courtship depends more on the reproductive cycles of the animals. Some pair up for life, while others stay together only for courtship and mating. Many birds perform courtship displays – noisy, colorful affairs in which the male birds show off their brightly colored feathers to impress the watching females. Females tend to have duller colors, to make them less obvious to predators when they are sitting on the nest and feeding their young. Male butterflies may be more brightly colored than females for similar reasons. In addition to colors and displays, ways of attracting a mate include scent and sound.

BUTTERFLY COLORS

Some male and female butterflies, such as these morphos (*left*), have very different colors. The shimmering colors of the male may play a part in attracting a female, but the way the wings reflect ultraviolet light also seems to be important. Male butterflies use scents as well as colors to attract females, and females seem to prefer the fittest males, the ones that are the strongest fliers.

BIRD OF PARADISE COURTSHIP DISPLAY

Some of the most spectacular courtship displays take place in the rain forests of New Guinea. Male birds of paradise, for example, perform elaborate displays (*right*); some even compete at communal display grounds, or leks, giving dazzling performances of color and sound. They often remove leaves just above their display grounds, so that a spotlight of sunshine draws attention to their spectacular dance.

COCK-OF-THE-ROCK

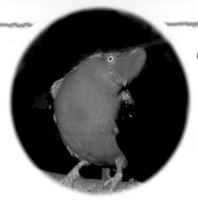

On a bare patch of the Amazon forest floor, the male cock-of-the-rock (*left*) displays to watching females, which have drab brown colors. He shows off by leaping into the air, bobbing his head, snapping his bill, and fanning out his feathers. He spreads his head crest forward so that it almost hides his bill. Females choose the males with the best display.

SMELLY MESSAGES

Female and male tigers live apart and come together only for mating. When a tigress is ready to mate, she leaves scent marks along the paths in her territory. This tigress (*left*) is leaving a scented message for a male tiger by rubbing scent glands on her face against tree bark. She also roars loudly to attract the attention of nearby males.

BOWERBIRDS

Instead of having bright, colorful feathers, male bowerbirds attract females by building an elaborate shelter, called a bower (*left*). Each bowerbird builds a different shape of bower from twigs woven together and decorated with colorful objects, such as shells, fruits, bones, pebbles, feathers, and flowers. Things thrown away by people, such as old bottle tops, sometimes end up decorating these bowers.

PARROT COURTSHIP

Before they mate, most male parrots display to the females by bowing, hopping, strutting, flicking their wings, and wagging their tails. They may also feed the female regurgitated food. In many species, the brightly colored irises of the eyes are expanded – a behavior pattern called eye blazing. Most parrots are monogamous, and males and females often pair up for life. They reinforce the bond between them by preening each other's feathers and feeding each other (*right*).

NESTS, EGGS, AND YOUNG

Although there is plenty of food and a variety of places to nest in a tropical rain forest, animals still have to compete for safe nesting sites and protect their eggs and young from predators. The forest's warm temperatures help the young to develop and survive the early, vulnerable stages of the life cycle, but the constant rain can make life miserable. Birds protect their eggs and young inside nests or tree holes, while marsupial mothers, such as tree kangaroos or possums, carry their young around with them for months in furry pouches. Even tarantulas guard their eggs until they hatch. But mammals, such as monkeys, cats, and bats, take the greatest care of their young, teaching them how to feed, hunt, and survive in the forest.

STRIPES AND SPOTS

Adult Brazilian tapirs are a plain brown color but the young have spots and stripes on their fur (*above*). The markings help to camouflage them so they blend into the background as they move through the light and shade of the rain forest. The markings also break up the outline of the young animal's body so it is harder to see.

BABY CARRIERS

Like their relatives that live on the ground, mother tree kangaroos have pouches to carry their young (*left*). The babies are born at a very early stage of their development. They crawl up to the pouch and fasten onto a teat to feed. Inside the pouch, the baby is warm and safe and can feed whenever it is hungry. It will spend several months there, completing its development.

HUMMINGBIRD NESTS

Most hummingbird nests (*right*) are small, open cups fixed to a twig by sticky cobwebs. The cups are deep and lined with moss and fluffy plant material to keep the eggs and young birds warm. Even after leaving the nest, the fledgling hummingbird is fed by its mother for as long as 20-40 days.

LIFE CYCLE OF AN OWL BUTTERFLY

A butterfly goes through four stages in its life cycle (*right*): egg, caterpillar (larva), pupa, and adult. In the warm climate of a tropical rain forest, a butterfly develops quickly and may complete its whole life cycle in just a few weeks.

Ribs and a tough coating on the eggs prevent them from drying out.

Young caterpillars have green skin; older ones have brown skin. Their function is to eat and grow bigger.

Inside the pupa, the caterpillar changes into a butterfly.

The role of the adult butterfly is reproduction and dispersal.

FROG TRANSPORTATION

Poison dart frogs usually lay their eggs on a leaf or a small area of ground they have carefully cleaned. One or both parents visit or guard the eggs until they hatch into tadpoles. Then a parent encourages the tadpoles to wriggle onto its back (*above*) and carries them to a stream or a pool of water among the leaves of a forest plant. Up to 35 tadpoles are carried in this way. The tadpoles do not fall off the adult's back because they are held there by a sticky secretion that breaks down only when under water.

CLINGING BABIES

A female orangutan usually gives birth to a single baby every three to six years. The baby rides on its mother's back or clings to her fur as she swings through the trees and sleeps in the same nest at night (*right*). Baby orangutans are totally dependent on their mothers for the first 18 months of their lives. Mothers do not mate again until their young are at least three years old, so a female may have only two or three babies during her lifetime.

LIVING TOGETHER

Social rain forest animals help each other spot predators, find food, and defend their young. In mammal societies where individuals live a long time, experienced older members of a group can help younger, inexperienced animals and teach them various survival skills. Mammal societies often have a "dominance hierarchy," where some are more important or high-ranking than others. Insect societies are highly organized, with groups of individuals carrying out different tasks.

ANT GARDENS

Colonies of leafcutter ants from Central American rain forests grow their own food in an underground nest. Worker ants bite off pieces of leaf and carry them back to the nest (*above*). There the leaves are chewed into small pieces, fertilized with the ants' droppings, and used to provide compost for growing fungi. The ants eat the fungus once it has grown. In some forests, leafcutter ants may eat over 15 percent of all the leaves grown.

TERMITE TOWERS

Tiny insects called termites build the equivalent of insect skyscrapers on the forest floor (*left*). These towers are made of tiny pieces of mud and saliva and take many years to construct. Millions of termites live in almost total darkness inside each tower. The queen termite lays the eggs, the workers look after the eggs and young and gather food, and soldier termites defend the nest.

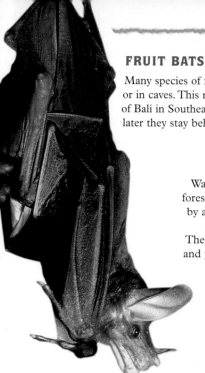

FRUIT BATS

Many species of fruit bat roost together in groups of hundreds of individuals on trees or in caves. This rousette fruit bat (*left*) is roosting in a cave on the Indonesian island of Bali in Southeast Asia. At first, young bats travel with their mother all the time, but later they stay behind in the roost while she goes out to hunt.

GORILLA GROUPS

Wandering slowly through the lowland and mountain forests of central Africa are small groups of gorillas, led by a dominant male. Mature male gorillas have silvery gray hair on their backs and are called silverbacks. They are too big and heavy to climb trees, but females and young are more agile and can climb up among the branches (*right*). Male gorillas defend the group from danger, but gorillas are intelligent, peaceful animals and all the members of a group play with the young.

SOUND SIGNALS

Gibbons, such as the siamang gibbon (*below*), live in monogamous family groups. The adult pairs in a group utter loud and complex calls, mainly as duets. These beautiful and haunting calls help to develop and maintain pair bonds and keep neighboring groups from invading each other's territory. Siamang gibbons stay very close to each other all the time.

GIRL POWER

In Central and South America, female and young coatis roam the forests in groups, or "bands," of up to 20 animals (*left*). They probe holes and cracks in the ground or in trees, searching for insects, spiders, and fruit. For most of the year the adult males live alone, but they are allowed to join the group for the few weeks of the mating period. Even then, the males are less important in the group than the females. After mating, the females soon drive the males away.

PEOPLES OF THE RAIN FOREST

NEW GUINEA PEOPLES

The New Guinea highlanders (*above*) decorate themselves in magnificent costumes for special occasions and perform complicated dances. They paint their faces and bodies in vivid colors. The patterns often relate to religious beliefs and ancestral spirits.

For thousands of years the world's tropical rain forests have been home to groups of people who have a deep and sensitive understanding of the forests. Their knowledge of local plants and animals, and their ability to use a wide range of foods and natural medicines, have made their survival possible, but population densities have never been high. Some rain forest peoples cultivate small patches of forest in a form of shifting cultivation. Unfortunately, as forests are cleared for their timber or their land, the homes of forest peoples are destroyed, or they die of diseases, such as influenza and measles, introduced by settlers from outside the forest.

SHIFTING CULTIVATION

In shifting cultivation, periods spent growing crops on a patch of land alternate with fallow periods when the land rests and recovers. In the common "slash-and-burn" version, which is well suited to the poor soils of a tropical rain forest, people cut down and burn a small area of forest (*right*), thereby destroying weeds and enriching the soil with plant nutrients. Then they plant seeds. As the crops grow, the plot needs constant weeding, since weeds grow well in the warm, wet conditions. Eventually, the weeds overcome the crops and the nutrients in the soil become used up, so the farmers move on to another patch of forest, leaving the cultivated area to lie fallow for 8 to 20 years. Shifting cultivation does not cause any lasting harm to the forest.

PYGMIES

The Pygmies of Africa (*left*) are adapted physically as well as culturally to their way of life as hunter-gatherers in the forest. Their small size makes it easier to move about in the undergrowth, and they have a light muscular build well suited to tree climbing. Some tribes of Pygmies seem to be completely at home in the treetops, often climbing to reach the nests of wild bees to collect honey. A small bird called a honeyguide often leads the hunters to a hive. The hunter helps the bird by opening the hive and leaves it a meal of beeswax as a reward.

NUMBERS OF PEOPLE

A large area of rain forest can support only a few hundred people – the population density of the Mbuti Pygmies is only about one person for every 1.5 square miles (4 sq km), and an individual band may range over as much as 500 square miles (1,300 sq km) in its search for food. So rain forest peoples are spread thinly through the forest. Some build houses to settle for a time (*right*); many families may live in the same house.

FOREST TRANSPORTATION

In dense forest it is easier to travel along rivers than through the undergrowth. Dugout canoes are often used for transportation, even today (*right*), but making them takes a long time. A tree has to be felled and then cut and hollowed out with an axe. Pieces of wood known as stretchers are placed across the canoe to keep it from warping. When the canoe is finished, a fire is lit underneath and inside it to harden and seal the wood.

HUNTING WEAPONS

This Mentawai man from Indonesia (*above*) is carrying his bow and arrow along with some stripped bark. To capture monkeys, birds, and other prey high in the canopy, rain forest hunter-gatherers use poisoned arrows or darts. The poisons come from plant juices or the skin of poisonous tree frogs. Sometimes hunters have to wait for hours before the prey dies and falls out of the trees.

CEREMONIES

Many tropical rain forest peoples paint their bodies with colorful dyes and use feathers, flowers, and other natural materials to make jewelry. Men, such as this Cofan Indian from Ecuador (*right*), are sometimes the only ones allowed to wear full ceremonial costume. There are strong traditions of dance and ceremony, and special occasions such as weddings, funerals, and harvests are marked by dances and feasts.

TIMBER!

Using chain saws, excavators, and other powerful machinery, logging companies can quickly clear huge areas of tropical rain forest (*above*). It takes several hundred years for a rain forest tree to grow taller than a power transmission tower, and only a few minutes for a man to chop it down with a chain saw. Roads have to be built to get the machinery into the forest, and since the valuable timber trees are scattered throughout the forest, great holes have to be torn in the forest to reach each one. Loggers usually destroy three times as many trees as they harvest.

PROTECTING THE RAIN FOREST

Tropical rain forests have taken millions of years to turn into the complex environments that they are today. They are very fragile because every part depends on every other part. Unfortunately, most rain forests are in poor, developing countries, which need to make money from timber, mineral resources (such as iron, copper, or uranium), or cash crops (such as coffee, cocoa, or bananas). Forest clearance causes many problems, among them soil erosion, floods, droughts, extinction of species, and disturbance of forest peoples. About half of all the tropical rain forests in the world have already been cut down, and about 2.5 acres (1 ha) of rain forest disappear every second. Much more could be done to save the world's rain forests. Timber companies could replace the trees they cut down, or maintain plantations of valuable rain forest trees. Trade in rare animal species could be controlled more effectively, and more large areas of rain forest could be preserved as national parks.

OUT INTO THE WILD

One way to help preserve endangered species is to breed the animals in captivity and then release them into the wild. But this is not a simple process. Since the released animals have never been in a natural rain forest, they need to learn how to survive, and this process of adjustment should be monitored. These golden lion tamarins (*left*) have been fitted with radio collars so scientists can follow their movements through the forest. In 1908 there were only about 100 golden lion tamarins in the wild, but conservation efforts have increased the number to about 500.

RAIN FOREST RESEARCH

Although rain forest people have a vast storehouse of knowledge about plants and animals in their forests, scientists also need to collect data to back up conservation projects. Millions of species need to be identified and the complex web of life better understood in order to figure out how best to preserve rain forests for the future. Because it is difficult to travel through the forest, some researchers float over it in airships (*right*) or take samples from the canopy using treetop rafts.

MEDICINAL PLANTS

These Antanosy girls (*right*) are holding a rosy periwinkle plant. It contains chemicals used in drugs for treating certain types of childhood leukemia and Hodgkin's disease, a form of lymphoma. The plant grows in the rapidly disappearing tropical rain forests of Madagascar and may soon become an endangered species. Many other rain forest plants may contain useful drugs, but they may become extinct before they are discovered. An estimated 20 percent of all drugs contain ingredients derived from tropical rain forest plants, but only about 1 percent of rain forest plants have been tested for possible use.

PROTECTED SPECIES

Large sums of money can be made from the trade in endangered animals and plants. There are international laws aimed at protecting rare species, but it is often difficult to enforce them. The Convention on International Trade in Endangered Species (CITES), which went into effect in 1975, protects jaguars (*right*), but illegal trade in jaguar skin is still carried on. Often the people who catch the animals make very little money from the trade, with the traders receiving most of the profit. One way to help limit the trade is for people to refuse to buy goods made from protected species.

FOR FURTHER INFORMATION

The followng are some of the sources available that can help you find out more about tropical rain forests and the plants, wildlife, and people living in them.

Books

Allaby, Michael, and Richard Garratt. *Tropical Rain Forests.* Biomes of the Earth series (Facts on File)
Butterfield, Moira. *Protecting Rain Forests* (Gareth Stevens)
Forsyth, Adrian. *Portraits of the Rainforest* (Camden House)
Goulding, Michael, and others. *The Smithsonian Atlas of the Amazon* (Smithsonian)
Kallen, Stuart A. *Rain Forests.* At Issue series (Greenhaven)
Knight, Tim. *Journey Into the Rainforest* (Oxford)
Luhr, James F. (editor). *Smithsonian Earth* (DK Publishing)

Web sites

Bagheera www.bagheera.com/
Forest Conservation Portal forests.org/
Learning About Rainforests www.srl.caltech.edu/personnel/krubal/rainforest/serve_home.html
Missouri Botanical Garden mbgnet.mobot.org/sets/rforest/
Mongabay www.mongabay.com/home.htm
Rainforest Alliance www.rainforest-alliance.org/
Rainforest Live www.rainforestlive.org.uk/
World Rainforest Information Portal www.rainforestweb.org/

Publisher's note to educators and parents: Our editors have carefully reviewed these Web sites to ensure that they are suitable for children. Many Web sites change frequently, however, and we cannot guarantee that a site's future contents will continue to meet our high standards of quality and educational value. Be advised that children should be closely supervised whenever they access the Internet.

Museums and zoos

American Museum of Natural History
Central Park West at 79th Street
New York, NY 10024

The Field Museum
1400 South Lake Shore Drive
Chicago, IL 60605-2496

Miami Museum of Science
3280 South Miami Avenue
Miami, FL 33129

Milwaukee Public Museum
800 West Wells Street
Milwaukee, WI 53233

National Museum of Natural History
10th Street and Constitution Avenue, NW
Washington, DC 20560-0166

Pana`ewa Rainforest Zoo
25 Aupuni South
Hilo, HI 96720-4245

GLOSSARY

algae: a group of simple plants that carry out photosynthesis and range from tiny microorganisms to huge seaweeds

adaptation: an evolutionary change in an organism in response to its environment

amphibians: a group of vertebrates (animals with a backbone) that spend their life partly on land and partly in water

bacteria: a group of single-celled microorganisms that lack a distinct cell nucleus

canopy: a forest's upper layer of leaves and branches

cyanobacteria: a group of bacteria that carry on photosynthesis; they were once called blue-green algae, although they are not actually algae

emergent: a tree so tall it rises above the forest's canopy

epiphyte: a plant that grows on another plant and gets its necessary water and nutrients from the air

food chain: a series of organisms that depend on each other for food

food web: a set of interacting food chains that exist in an ecological community

lichen: a complex life-form consisting of a fungus plus an organism that can perform photosynthesis – algae or the type of bacteria known as cyanobacteria

mammals: a group of vertebrates (animals with a backbone) that nourish their young on milk produced by the mother

marsupials: a group of mammals whose young are born at an early stage of development and then continue to mature while carried in a pouch on the mother's body; most modern marsupials are found in Australasia

photosynthesis: a sunlight-based process used by green plants and some microorganisms to make water and carbon dioxide into food

prehensile: capable of gripping or grasping something; some animals, for example, have prehensile tails

pollen: fine grains made by a seed plant that fertilize egg cells, causing them to develop into seeds

predator: an organism that kills other organisms for food

prey: a creature killed for food by a predator

temperate rain forest: a rain forest located not in the tropics but in the temperate climate zone; temperate rain forests tend to have less diversity of life-forms than tropical rain forests, as well as greater diversity of temperature over the course of the year

understory: the layer of a forest between the canopy and the ground layer at the forest floor

water cycle: the continuous movement of water between the Earth's atmosphere and its surface: rain or other precipitation falls from the sky on the land (including plants) and sea; some of the water evaporates back into the air from plants, the land, and the sea

INDEX

2321081